SOUTH CAROLINA

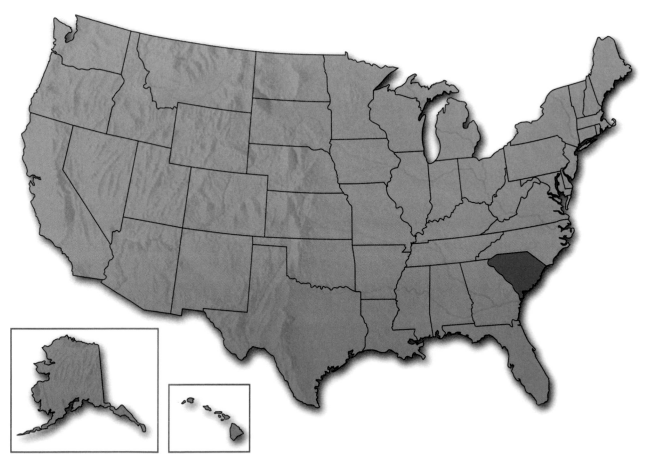

Janice Parker

Published by Weigl Publishers Inc.
123 South Broad Street, Box 227
Mankato, MN   56002
USA
Web site: http://www.weigl.com

Library of Congress Cataloging-in-Publication Data available upon
request from the publisher. Fax: (507) 388-2746 for the attention of the
Publishing Records Department.

ISBN 1-930954-59-X

Printed in the United States of America
1 2 3 4 5 6 7 8 9 10   05 04 03 02 01

Editor
Jennifer Nault
Copy Editor
Kara Turner
Designers
Warren Clark
Terry Paulhus
Layout
Bryan Pezzi
Photo Researcher
Diana Marshall

Photograph Credits
Every reasonable effort has been made to trace ownership and to obtain
permission to reprint copyright material. The publishers would be
pleased to have any errors or omissions brought to their attention so
that they may be corrected in subsequent printings.

Cover: beach (Courtesy of Hilton Head Island Chamber of Commerce), palmetto
(Corel Corporation); **Jay Browne Photography:** page 7T; **Cheraw Visitors Bureau:**
pages 13B, 21B; **Corel Corporation:** pages 4BL, 9B, 10B, 11T, 11ML, 14T, 29T; **Digital
Stock:** page 8B; **Digital Vision Ltd.:** page 9T; **Courtesy of the Hilton Head Island
Chamber of Commerce:** page 11B; **Hulton/Archive:** pages 17, 21T, 27T; **©Bob
Krist/Corbis/Magma:** page 23B; **Myrtle Beach Area Chamber of Commerce:** pages
5T, 7B, 10T, 12T, 15T, 20T, 20BR, 28L, 28R, 29BL; **Pee Dee Tourism Commission:**
pages 15B, 27B; **PhotoDisc, Inc.:** page 14BR; **Photofest:** pages 25T, 25B; **J & D
Richardson:** pages 4BR, 8T, 13T, 24T; **Sonoco Products Company:** page 14BL; **South
Carolina Department of Parks, Recreation & Tourism:** pages 3T, 3M, 3B, 4T, 6T, 6B,
12B, 20BL, 22T, 22B, 23T, 24B, 26T, 26BL, 26BR; **Courtesy of South Caroliniana
Library, University of South Carolina, Columbia:** pages 16T,16B,18T,18B,19T, 9B.

CONTENTS

INTRODUCTION

The popular Grand Strand is a 60-mile stretch of white-sand beach, which runs along the South Carolina coast from Little River to Georgetown.

There can be no doubt that the motto found on license plates in South Carolina—"Smiling Faces, Beautiful Places"—suits this wonderful state. Living in a state so rich in history and culture gives residents much to smile about. As one of the original thirteen colonies to form the United States, South Carolina has a long and interesting history. South Carolina has also made great strides in the jazz and blues music scenes. For instance, legendary jazz trumpeter Dizzy Gillespie hails from this southern state.

South Carolina is the location of many "Beautiful Places." As part of the Deep South, it is blessed with a beautiful, varied landscape and a warm climate. South Carolina's mountains and seashore attract many tourists to the state. In fact, Myrtle Beach, one of the nation's top vacation spots, draws about 13 million visitors annually.

One of South Carolina's most visited historical attractions is the Magnolia Plantation and Gardens, which are home to a varied tropical plant life and a 125-acre waterfowl refuge.

QUICK FACTS

South Carolina is called the "Palmetto State."

The state flag was created during the American Revolution by Colonel William Moultrie, in 1775, for his troops. The crescent represents the silver emblems on the soldiers' caps. Later, a palmetto tree was added to the center of the flag to represent the brave defense of the palmetto-log fort on Sullivan's Island by Moultrie and his troops.

The Myrtle Beach International Airport is just 3 miles away from Myrtle Beach's oceanfront.

Getting There

The state of South Carolina is triangle-shaped. It is bordered by North Carolina to the north and northeast, Georgia to the west and southwest, and the Atlantic Ocean to the east.

People can access the state in a variety of ways, but air travel is often the fastest mode of transportation. South Carolina has four major airports: the Charleston International Airport, the Greenville-Spartanburg, the Columbia Metropolitan Airport, and, lastly, the Myrtle Beach International Airport.

For automobile travelers, South Carolina has about 64,000 miles of roads and highways. Seven railroads provide freight service in the state, and about ten cities are served by passenger trains.

QUICK FACTS

South Carolina is in the eastern standard time zone, which is five hours behind Greenwich mean time. The state observes daylight-saving time between April and October.

The state motto, *Dum Spiro Spero*, means "While I Breathe, I Hope" in Latin.

The Columbia Metropolitan Airport is the state's largest airport. It covers 2,600 acres and handles more than 1 million passengers each year.

More than 1,400 people work at the Columbia Metropolitan Airport.

Johnston, South Carolina is known as the "Peach Capital of the World."

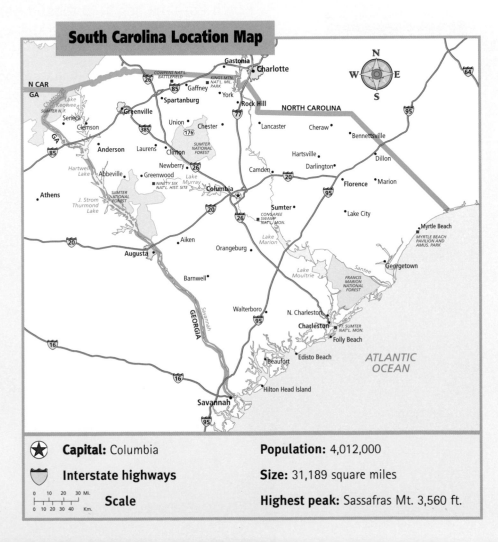

South Carolina Location Map

⭐ **Capital:** Columbia

🛡 **Interstate highways**

Scale
0 10 20 30 Mi.
0 10 20 30 40 Km.

Population: 4,012,000

Size: 31,189 square miles

Highest peak: Sassafras Mt. 3,560 ft.

The well-known Battery area in Charleston is lined with grand historic houses that face Fort Sumter.

QUICK FACTS

South Carolina is 31,189 square miles in size, making it the fortieth-largest state in the nation. Its total area includes 1,006 square miles of inland water and 72 square miles of coastal waters.

The state was the site of many battles during the American Revolution. The English captured the city of Charleston in 1780.

About one quarter of the 63,000 troops from South Carolina were killed during the American Civil War.

The English first settled in South Carolina in 1670. They named their settlement Charles Town. For much of its early history, South Carolina was ruled by a wealthy colonial society. Many colonists owned **plantations** and grew crops, such as rice and cotton.

In 1850, a dispute between the northern and the southern states arose over the issue of slavery. While much of the North opposed slavery, the South wanted to keep the plantation culture. On December 20, 1860, South Carolina became the first state to **secede** from the Union.

The American Civil War began on April 12, 1861, when Confederate troops fired upon Fort Sumter in Charleston Harbor. During the war, South Carolina's coast was the site of much fighting. When the Union **blockaded** Charleston Harbor, South Carolina's economy crashed. Then, in 1865, Union troops destroyed many of the state's plantations. Union troops also burned Columbia, the state capital. After the war, South Carolina began to rebuild its economy. New industries, such as textiles, helped pave the way to a brighter future.

Historic re-enactments, staged in traditional battle uniforms, replay the battles that took place on South Carolina's soil during the American Revolution.

South Carolina's capital, Columbia, was founded on March 26, 1786. This center of government, education, and commerce was named for the explorer, Christopher Columbus.

Today, buildings that date back to before the American Civil War can still be seen in such cities as Beaufort and Charleston. Large plantations also exist in parts of South Carolina. The state's beautiful flower gardens, blooming with flowers, such as magnolias, are fragrant reminders of early colonial life in South Carolina.

Once based primarily upon agriculture, South Carolina gradually moved toward an industry-based economy. Today, manufacturing is one of the most significant industries in South Carolina. Most South Carolinians work in the service industry, which includes retail, health care, and government. With its natural beauty and fascinating history, tourism is also booming in the Palmetto State.

QUICK FACTS

The state capital of South Carolina is Columbia. The city was chosen in 1786 because it was near the center of the state.

South Carolina's Atlantic coastline is approximately 187 miles long. But the state has 2,876 miles of coastline if all the bays, inlets, and islands are included.

South Carolina was the eighth state to **ratify** the United States Constitution.

Before being known as "The Palmetto State," South Carolina was known as "The Iodine State."

There is a water storage tank in the shape of a peach in Gaffney.

Murrells Inlet, nicknamed "The Seafood Capital of South Carolina," can be observed while strolling the 1,400-foot Marshwalk, which winds along the wetlands of this harbor village.

At an elevation of 3,208 feet, the Caesar's Head Overlook rises above the Carolina Piedmont.

LAND AND CLIMATE

South Carolina has three distinct land regions: the Atlantic Coastal Plain, the Piedmont, and the Blue Ridge region, a tiny area in the northwestern portion of the state. The Blue Ridge Mountains extend from Virginia to Georgia. The highest peak in the mountain range is Sassafras Mountain, which lies on the border between North and South Carolina. South Carolina also includes thirteen major islands and many smaller ones. The three major rivers of South Carolina are the Santee River, which at 143 miles in length is the longest river that falls entirely within the state, the Savannah River, and the Great Pee Dee River. Surprisingly, there are no large natural lakes in the state. Still, many artificial lakes have been created by damming the major rivers.

South Carolina has a subtropical climate with hot, humid summers and mild winters. The state experiences ten tornadoes, on average, each year.

The hurricane season in South Carolina is from June to November. In September of 1989, the state had an unwelcome visitor. Hurricane Hugo blasted the coast with 130-mile-an-hour winds.

South Carolina has a strong forest industry. Forests cover approximately 12.6 million acres of the state.

NATURAL RESOURCES

Natural resources in South Carolina include rich soils, minerals, vast forests, and an abundant water supply. About two-thirds of South Carolina is forested. More than 90 percent of all forests in the state are privately owned. The state ranks sixth in the nation in the production of pulpwood.

Many minerals used in construction and other industries are mined in South Carolina, including clay, granite, limestone, vermiculite, and kaolin. South Carolina is ranked second in the nation in the production of kaolin, a white clay mineral. Only Georgia produces more kaolin. There are about thirty kaolin mines in the state. Kaolin is used in many products, including paper, vehicle tires, paint, and cosmetics. Limestone was first mined in South Carolina in the 1820s. Limestone is one of the main ingredients of portland cement. South Carolina produces about $118 million of cement each year.

QUICK FACTS

Vermiculite is a mineral that expands to twenty times its size when it is heated. There are twenty-nine vermiculite mines in South Carolina. The state produces and sells more of this mineral than any other state.

South Carolina was the only gold-producing state east of the Mississippi River until 1999. The Kennecott Ridgeway Mining Company mine began producing gold in 1988. The area is now being reclaimed for recreational use.

Granite is a rock that is primarily used in the construction industry. It was first mined in South Carolina around 1786.

Six percent of South Carolina's total work force are in construction.

PLANTS AND ANIMALS

The cabbage palmetto, also known as the Inodes palmetto and the Sabal palmetto, was chosen as the South Carolina state tree on March 17, 1939.

Loblolly and longleaf pine trees are common throughout South Carolina forests. Other trees include oak, cypress, magnolia, elm, sycamore, and tupelo. The state tree, the cabbage palmetto, grows along the coast. The cabbage palmetto is an evergreen palm tree that can grow up to 33 feet in height. The leaves can be as large as 3 feet across. Raccoons, robins, and other birds feed on the fruit of the tree. The large leaf bud of the cabbage palmetto is edible and is used in salads, pickles, and relishes. Some people also eat part of the stem, which tastes like cabbage. During the American Revolution, palmetto logs were used to build forts along the coast. The soft trunks did not break when they were struck by cannonballs.

Flowering shrubs and wildflowers grow throughout the state, including the yellow jessamine and flowering dogwood. Mountain laurel and various types of rhododendron grow in mountain regions.

Along the shaded banks of the streams in the Cliffs at Glassy Preserve, rhododendron thickets outnumber all other plants.

QUICK FACTS

The yellow jessamine became the official state flower on February 1, 1924. The flower had long been a favorite of South Carolinians. The Dixie Chapter of the United Daughters of Confederacy chose the yellow jessamine as their floral emblem in 1906.

South Carolina and North Carolina are the only places in the world where the Venus's-flytrap grows wild.

Pitcher plants grow wild in South Carolina. They have hooded, pitcher-shaped leaves containing a liquid that traps insects.

spotted salamander

Common wild animals in the state include white-tailed deer, beavers, and squirrels. More than 360 species of birds have been spotted in South Carolina. Hawks, owls, and bald eagles make their home in the state. Other native birds include the swallow, Baltimore oriole, and pelican. South Carolina's coast is part of the Atlantic Flyway, a north–south route used by many species of birds during their annual migration.

Turtles, lizards, salamanders, frogs, and toads can be found in swamp areas. Alligators live in the coastal regions. The largest reptile in North America, the American alligator, lives in the lakes, streams, and swamps of South Carolina. The American alligator can be as long as 20 feet. It is black with yellow bands of color that fade with age. This alligator can be dangerous, especially if humans trespass upon its habitat.

In answer to the growing number of alligator encounters with humans, South Carolina has recently initiated a program allowing controlled hunting on private lands. This helps control alligator populations.

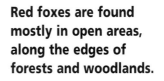

Red foxes are found mostly in open areas, along the edges of forests and woodlands.

At Alligator Adventure in Myrtle Beach, visitors can get close to exotic animals such as the rare albino American alligator.

QUICK FACTS

About 3 percent of the visitors to South Carolina come from outside the United States.

South Carolina has two national forests, the Sumter and the Francis Marion, and forty-seven state parks.

The American Military Museum in Charleston has exhibits that represent all the major wars in which the United States has been involved.

The island of Hilton Head, which at 42 square miles is the largest island in South Carolina, is home to four large tourist resorts. The island also boasts more than 300 tennis courts and more than 20 golf courses.

South Carolina's state beverage is milk, and its hospitality beverage is tea.

TOURISM

Known for its warm climate, lush mountains, long coastline, and friendly people, South Carolina is a popular tourist destination. In fact, more than 28 million people traveled to South Carolina in 2000. Many people come to discover the Grand Strand area, which enjoys more than 200 sunny days each year. It is here that Myrtle Beach is found.

Tourism brings $7 billion into South Carolina every year, supporting about 115,600 jobs. There are many attractions that draw visitors to the state. History buffs can travel to Charleston, where they can tour buildings from the Colonial period. Charleston is also home to many museums, including the Confederate Museum, which displays artifacts, such as uniforms and pistols, from the Confederate Army.

Charleston's Magnolia Plantation and Gardens, which was founded in 1676, is the oldest public garden in the United States. On the plantation grounds is the Barbados Tropical Garden—the oldest garden in the United States. The Barbados Tropical Garden is a tribute to the country of origin of the gardens' first owners.

At Myrtle Beach, tourists enjoy the surf and sand, as well as theaters, shopping, golfing, and an old-fashioned amusement park.

Located in Charleston, Shem Creek is home to a large shrimping fleet.

INDUSTRY

Agriculture was the backbone of South Carolina's economy in the early 1900s. Although agriculture is still important to the state, many more South Carolinians now work in the manufacturing and service industries. Manufacturing is the most important economic activity in the state. Many of the nation's top corporations have manufacturing facilities in South Carolina, including General Motors, Exxon, Wal-Mart, and General Electric.

The state's leading agricultural products are tobacco, peaches, and soybeans. South Carolina is the second-largest producer in the nation of peaches and flue-cured tobacco. Grown primarily in the Pee Dee region, tobacco accounts for nearly one-quarter of all income earned from crops in South Carolina. Other leading crops include cotton, wheat, and corn.

Freshly picked South Carolina cotton is emptied into a module builder. Thousands of compressed cotton modules are then taken to a gin for cleaning.

QUICK FACTS

There are about 25,000 farms in South Carolina.

The boll weevil, a type of beetle, damaged many cotton crops in South Carolina during the 1920s. As a result, farmers began raising other crops, such as fruit, tobacco, and wheat.

In 1998, the fishing industry earned $28.3 million. Shrimp, crab, clams, and oysters are the most important commercial products.

The peach is the state fruit of South Carolina.

COTTON BUGGY

South Carolina's textile industry manufactures carpets for homes, along with other items.

GOODS AND SERVICES

Chemicals are the leading manufactured products in South Carolina. The main products in this category include **synthetic** fibers, plastic resins, dyes, and **pharmaceuticals**. The main centers for chemical production are Greenville, Spartanburg, Columbia, and Charleston.

Textile production is also a significant industry in South Carolina. The state has 350 textile factories, and one-quarter of the state's manufacturing workers are employed by textile companies. Milliken & Company, which is headquartered in Spartanburg, is one of the nation's largest textile companies. The company has the largest textile research center in the world, and holds more than 1,300 **patents**. Worldwide, Milliken & Company employs 16,000 people. Mount Vernon, a textile company based in Greenville, is another of the nation's leading textile firms. The company, which dates back to the 1830s, has seventeen manufacturing plants. Cotton fabrics are the most significant textile products, but South Carolina also produces yarn, carpet, and synthetic fabrics, such as nylon and rayon.

Chemical production contributes more than 10 percent to the state's industrial income.

Myrtle Beach has more than 100 hotels and resort rental properties, which provide jobs for local South Carolinians.

About 2 million South Carolinians are members of the work force, and 25 percent of them work in the service industry. Retail or wholesale trade workers make up 22 percent of the work force, while 17 percent are in manufacturing, and 17 percent work for the government. The rest work in areas such as finance, construction, transportation, farming, forestry, and mining.

South Carolina has numerous educational facilities for higher learning. The University of South Carolina, which opened in 1801, has more than 35,000 students enrolled. The University of South Carolina offers more than 375 degree programs for its students. South Carolina has been working to improve their education system. The state passed the Education Improvement Act, in 1984, to raise standards and provide increased funding for education.

South Carolina has thirty-five school districts and about eighty-four secondary schools within those districts.

QUICK FACTS

Greenville is home to the North American Michelin headquarters. Michelin manufactures tires. The company has more than 130,000 employees worldwide.

Forest products bring more than $572 million into the state each year.

The South Carolina State Library's general collection holds about 240,000 books.

Fifty-eight percent of the electricity produced in South Carolina is generated by nuclear power plants. The state has seven nuclear plants. Another 39 percent of the state's electricity comes from coal-fueled steam plants.

South Carolina has fifteen daily newspapers and more than seventy weekly newspapers. The state also has about 24 television stations and 185 radio stations.

In the 1740s, Sir Alexander Cuming was involved in the creation of a treaty which stated that Native Peoples in the South Carolina area would only trade with the English.

QUICK FACTS

In 1993, the federal government officially recognized the Catawba's land claims. They were given $50 million and 144,000 acres of land in York County. Today, about 1,400 Catawba live in South Carolina on a 640-acre reservation near Rock Hill.

Many South Carolina place names are derived from Native-American words, such as Awendaw, Pocotaligo, Tamassee, Seneca, and Yemassee.

In 1838 and 1839, as many as 20,000 Cherokee were forced to leave their homes and travel to Oklahoma on foot. During this march, called the Trail of Tears, at least 4,000 Cherokee died.

FIRST NATIONS

Native Peoples have lived in the South Carolina region for more than 10,000 years. Around 2000 BC, the Native Peoples began to plant crops, such as corn and squash. About 900 years ago, a cultural group called the Mound Builders flourished in the region. Much later, in the 1600s, about thirty different groups of 15,000 Native Peoples were living in the South Carolina region. The Cherokee, who spoke an Iroquoian language, lived in the Up Country areas of the state. The Cherokee lived in villages and made homes from small trees, mud, and bark. The Catawba also lived in the Up Country. They spoke a Siouan language and were known for their tradition of making pottery. Early Catawba potters worked with clay, which was sometimes mixed with Spanish moss and rolled into coils before being formed into bowls.

Today, the largest Native-American group in South Carolina is the Pee Dee. There are more than 2,500 Pee Dee in the state, and most live in the northeast.

During the 1600s, the Yemassee lived in the Low Country, along the coast of South Carolina. After the 1715 war against the English, the Yemassee moved to Florida.

EXPLORERS AND MISSIONARIES

In 1526, when Lucas Vásquez de Ayllón founded a colony in South Carolina, he brought along Francisco Chicora to act as a guide and interpreter. Chicora was one of the Native Peoples taken by Francisco Gordillo as a slave. He escaped from his captors soon after they arrived in South Carolina.

Spanish explorers established the city of Santa Elena on Parris Island in 1566. Nearly 500 Spaniards lived in the city, which was the capital of Spanish Florida from 1568 to 1576. In 1856, the English forced the Spaniards out of Santa Elena.

In 1520, Francisco Gordillo led an expedition that explored the coast of South Carolina. He stopped to trade goods with the Native Peoples along the coast. When he left, he took more than 100 Native Peoples with him as slaves. In 1526, Lucas Vásquez de Ayllón, another Spanish explorer, came to South Carolina with about 600 people. He started a colony near Georgetown. The colony faced many difficulties. Illness, poor relations with the Native Peoples, and bad weather forced the group to travel home after just a few months.

In 1562, the French tried unsuccessfully to start a colony on Parris Island. Captain Jean Ribaut and a small group of French Huguenots built a fort there. Soon after, Ribaut returned to France to get more men and supplies. When he did not return, the settlers, with the help of the Native Peoples, built a ship and attempted to sail home. The French Huguenots experienced difficulties at sea and were saved by English sailors. Eventually, they returned to France.

F. Delfinum

Many French Huguenots sailed to South Carolina after the Catholic Church called for their execution in 1535.

EARLY SETTLERS

King Charles I ruled Great Britain for 11 years.

In 1629, King Charles I of England granted parts of North America to Sir Robert Heath. This area included a strip of land covering what are now the states of South Carolina and North Carolina. King Charles I decided to call the region south of Virginia, Carolana. *Carolana* means "land of Charles" in Latin. In 1663, the name was changed slightly, to Carolina. In 1670, 148 colonists became the first settlers in South Carolina. Many of the them had been living on the island of Barbados. They called their settlement Charles Town, after King Charles II. Ten years later, the settlement was moved across the river to a better location. This is the location of present-day Charleston.

By 1700, about 5,000 settlers were living in the area. The population included some French Huguenots, who arrived from New England. The French Huguenots were Protestants who left France to escape religious **persecution**. Many moved to other European countries, or to North America, where they were free to practice their religion.

Early Charleston grew rapidly in population, commerce, shipping, and culture due mainly to its harbor location.

South Carolina rice laborers were each responsible for 5 acres of rice.

In 1712, Carolina was split into North Carolina and South Carolina. In 1729, South Carolina officially became a royal province of England. By the following year, the state was home to about 30,000 settlers, mostly living in or around Charles Town.

During the middle of the eighteenth century, a rivalry began between people living in the Low Country, mostly residents of Charles Town, and people who lived in the Up Country. Low Country residents were often wealthy plantation owners. Much of their land was cultivated by African Americans who were made to work as slaves. The Up Country, on the other hand, was populated by small farm owners who did not own slaves.

During the 1700s, rice and indigo were grown throughout the state. Indigo, a plant that produces a blue pigment, was used to dye cloth. South Carolinians grew large quantities of indigo and sold it to England. In 1775, about 1 million pounds of indigo were exported from South Carolina.

Indigo production involved intensive manual labor. It also required a high degree of technical skill.

POPULATION

The population of South Carolina is about 4 million. About 67 percent of the population is of European descent, while nearly 30 percent is African American. Twelve percent of the population is aged 65 years or older, and about 25 percent of the population is below the age of 18. This age distribution is similar to the national average. About 36 percent of the population over the age of 25 hold a high school diploma, while 10 percent has a college degree.

Historically, South Carolina has been a mostly **rural** population. Today, 55 percent of South Carolinians live in **urban** areas. South Carolina has a population density of 133 people per square mile—this number is significantly higher than the national average of about 80 people per square mile. The largest city in South Carolina is Columbia, with a population of 110,840.

From 1990 to 1998, approximately 20,000 people migrated to Horry County, which includes Myrtle Beach.

Young residents of South Carolina flock to its many beaches during school break.

QUICK FACTS

The five largest cities in South Carolina are Columbia, Charleston, North Charleston, Greenville, and Rock Hill.

The U.S. Census Bureau estimates that South Carolina will have a population of more than 4.6 million by the year 2025.

More than 98 percent of South Carolinians were born in the United States.

POLITICS AND GOVERNMENT

South Carolina is governed by its state constitution, which was adopted in 1895. The South Carolina government has three branches: the executive branch, the legislative branch, and the judicial branch. The state governor, who is elected to a four-year term, heads the executive branch. The executive branch includes several other elected officials, including the lieutenant governor, the secretary of state, and the attorney general. The state legislature is called the General Assembly and includes a House of Representatives with 124 members and a Senate with 46 members. Representatives are elected for two-year terms, while senators are elected for four-year terms. The judicial branch is the state court system. The highest court is the Supreme Court. This court is headed by a chief **justice** and four associate justices.

Reverend Jesse Jackson, a political and civil-rights leader, was born in Greenville in 1941.

QUICK FACTS

Reverend Jesse Jackson helped bring racial and economic equality by founding groups such as the National Rainbow Coalition.

South Carolina is divided into 46 counties. The state has more than 270 separate municipalities, most of which are governed by a mayor and a city council.

The seventh president of the United States, Andrew Jackson, was born in South Carolina in 1767. Andrew Jackson was known for his democratic beliefs.

South Carolina sends six representatives and two senators to the U.S. Congress and has eight electoral votes.

Members of the General Assembly elect Supreme Court judges to terms of 10 years.

Cheraw's historic town hall, built in 1858, is still used for city offices.

The state is renowned for its unique southern-style cooking, which uses seafood as a key ingredient. Southern cooking is often very spicy.

QUICK FACTS

In 1983, South Carolina elected the first African-American state senator to be elected in the twentieth century— I. DeQuincey Newman.

The Civil Rights Act of 1964 put an end to **segregation** laws in all public facilities. This act also allowed more African Americans to vote. The percentage of African Americans registered to vote in South Carolina more than doubled to almost 39 percent.

In the 1800s, the Mann-Simons Cottage was used by many African-American church groups in Columbia. The house was saved from demolition in the 1970s, and is preserved today as a tribute to the Mann and Simons families.

CULTURAL GROUPS

Five out of the original 148 people to settle in South Carolina were from Africa. Soon, many more Africans were brought to South Carolina and forced to work as slaves.

In 1685, English settlers attempted to cultivate rice in South Carolina. They had little luck. African Americans, who had grown rice in Africa, showed the English how to grow rice in wet areas. So began the rice culture, which made many South Carolinians very wealthy. Unfortunately, the practice of slavery would exist for many years to follow.

Today, African Americans in South Carolina have overcome great odds and have worked toward achieving racial and economic equality. Some museums in the state showcase cultural artifacts relating to African Americans in South Carolina. The Mann-Simons Cottage, in Columbia, houses the Museum of African-American Culture. The cottage was purchased in the mid-1800s, by Celia Mann, a slave who had bought her own freedom.

Gospel music, spiritual music with African-American roots, became popular in the 1930s.

Sweetgrass basket weavers use strips of sweetgrass, marsh bulrush, and long-leaf pine needles.

QUICK FACTS

The Gullah language
is spoken with a unique rhythm and at a quick pace.

The Native Islander Gullah Celebration,
on the island of Hilton Head, showcases the music, food, crafts, and history of the island. Events include an art exhibition, a gospel concert, and an old-fashioned barbecue.

The Gullah Festival,
a five-day celebration of Gullah culture, takes place in Beaufort each year. The festival highlights Gullah food, dancers, arts and crafts, storytelling, and music.

The Gullah came from Sierra Leone in West Africa. They were first brought to South Carolina to work as slaves in the early seventeenth century. Many of the Gullah communities in South Carolina were located on small islands and separated from the rest of the state. The Gullah had their own unique culture, which included traditional storytelling, special fish and rice dishes, and crafts. The Gullah are particularly known for their woven grass baskets. The term "Gullah" also refers to a distinct creole language, which is a blend of African and English languages. Today, very few people speak Gullah.

The Gullah live in communities near Charleston, Hilton Head, and Georgetown. The island lifestyle of the Gullah is rich in heritage. Traditional Gullah storytelling, cooking, and crafts bring visitors to the Charleston area. The Charleston sweetgrass basket, a 1,000-year-old art form, is still made in the area. Visitors to Charleston's Market can watch Gullah people crafting baskets with traditional weaving tools made out of bone.

Drums and the traditional Gullah "shout" play a central role in the music of the Gullah culture.

George Farquhar's *The Recruiting Officer* **was the first performance to open in the Dock Street Theatre, on February 12, 1736.**

QUICK FACTS

Many feature films have been made in South Carolina, including *Forrest Gump, The Prince of Tides,* and *Days of Thunder.*

From 1734 to 1735, Charleston staged the first opera in what was to become the United States. The first symphony orchestra in the nation also began in South Carolina.

Both Charleston and Columbia have symphony orchestras.

Poet James Dickey lived most of his life in South Carolina.

Batesburg-Leesville is home to the annual South Carolina Poultry Festival, held in early May.

ARTS AND ENTERTAINMENT

South Carolina is home to many fine art museums. The South Carolina State Museum in Columbia has an extensive collection of South Carolina art, as well as other exhibits on history and science. The museum is housed in the old Columbia Mill, which has been standing since 1893. The Charleston Museum—the nation's first museum—was founded in 1773. Its aim is to preserve the natural and cultural history of South Carolina. The Children's Museum of South Carolina, at Myrtle Beach, allows young people to learn by exploring and playing with **interactive** exhibits.

South Carolina has a long history of theater. The state boasts the nation's first building designed solely for theatrical performances. In 1736, the Dock Street Theatre opened in Charleston. The theater burned down in the Great Fire of 1740, a blaze that destroyed the city's French quarter. A hotel was built on the site in 1809. Much later, in 1937, the building was restored and reopened as the Dock Street Theatre. Each year, more than 100,000 people attend performances at the Dock Street Theatre.

The Spoleto Festival U.S.A. is a major performing arts festival held in Charleston each spring. It was established in 1977 and features dance, theater, music, and visual arts.

John Birks Gillespie earned the nickname "Dizzy" for his comical stage antics and cool attitude.

Author Pat Conroy was born in Georgia, but moved to South Carolina at a young age. In 1972, Conroy published a novel called *The Water is Wide*. In it, he related his experiences teaching young African-American students who were living in poverty. The National Education Association honored Conroy with a humanitarian award for the book, which was later made into the film, *Conrack*. Conroy's best-known novel is *The Prince of Tides*, published in 1986. This highly acclaimed novel was made into a film starring Barbra Streisand and Nick Nolte.

Jazz trumpeter and composer Dizzy Gillespie was born in Cheraw in 1917. Along with Charlie Parker, Gillespie is considered to be one of the founders of the bebop movement in jazz. Bebop is a style of jazz based on **improvisation** and was developed in the 1940s. Singer and performer Eartha Kitt was born in North in 1928. When she was young, Kitt toured the world as a dancer with the Katherine Dunham Dance Troupe. She is best known for her work on Broadway and has acted in a variety of television shows and films, such as the 1960s television program, *Batman*. In 1996, Kitt appeared in the children's movie, *Harriett the Spy*.

QUICK FACTS

Many great writers have come from South Carolina, including Julia Peterkin. She won the Pulitzer Prize for Literature in 1928.

Painter Jasper Johns, a well-known **pop artist**, grew up in South Carolina.

Born in Charleston, writer DuBose Heywards's most successful novel was *Porgy*. It was published in 1925. The novel served as the inspiration for George Gershwin's famous opera, *Porgy and Bess*.

The South Carolina Apple Festival celebrates the beginning of apple harvest season in Oconee County.

In *Batman*, Eartha Kitt sharpened her claws as the coy villain, Catwoman.

Pete Dye, well-known for his golf-course architecture, built South Carolina's Harbor Town Golf Links in 1969.

QUICK FACTS

Althea Gibson was born near Sumter in 1927. In 1957, she became the first African-American tennis player to win Wimbledon. She won the championship again in 1958.

About 10 million people visit South Carolina's state parks each year to camp, hike, fish, and swim. One-quarter of the visitors come from out of the state.

SPORTS

South Carolina's varied landscape and warm climate are perfectly suited to all types of outdoor recreation. With forty-six state parks, camping and hiking are year-round activities in South Carolina. Boating, sailing, and swimming are popular in coastal areas. Water-skiing, **parasailing**, canoeing, and kayaking are other water sports that are enjoyed in the state.

South Carolina is one of the premier golfing states in the nation. There are golf courses in every region of the state. The Heritage Head Classic Golf Tournament is held each year on Hilton Head Island.

Steeplechase is a popular spectator sport in the state. The Carolina Cup, established in 1930, is hailed as South Carolina's largest sporting event. More than 50,000 fans come to Camden's Springdale Race Track to watch this thrilling sport each year. Spectators come to watch thoroughbred horses racing at 35 miles per hour over 5-foot-high fences. The Carolina Cup presents the best of steeplechase.

Aiken hosts the Aiken Triple Crown every year. This event includes three weekends of horse racing events: the Aiken Trials, the Aiken Steeplechase, and the Harness Races.

QUICK FACTS

Born in Columbia,
Alex English played fifteen seasons in the National Basketball Association (NBA). He played in eight NBA all-star games and was the NBA scoring champion in 1983. He was inducted into the Baseball Hall of Fame in 1998.

Boxing legend
Joe Frazier was born in Beaufort in 1944.

About 600,000 people
hold hunting and fishing licenses in South Carolina.

The South Carolina Stingrays, established in 1993, are the farm team for the Buffalo Sabres of the National Hockey League.

The only major league
baseball player to wear the name of his hometown on his uniform was pitcher Bill Voiselle, from Ninety Six, South Carolina. He wore the number 96 on his jersey.

The era of NASCAR speedway racing began at the Darlington Raceway on September 4, 1950. This oval raceway has been billed as "Too Tough To Tame." Darlington attracts many visitors to the NASCAR TranSouth Financial 400 stock-car race in the spring and the Mountain Dew Southern 500 race during Labor Day weekend. While at the raceway, people can visit the Stock Car Hall of Fame–Joe Weatherly Museum. The museum houses a large collection of historic race cars and driver memorabilia.

Larry Doby played center field for the Cleveland Indians.

College sports, in particular football and basketball, are popular in South Carolina. Although South Carolina does not have any professional sports teams, many South Carolinians have played professional sports. Aiken native William Perry, nicknamed "The Refrigerator," was a defensive lineman for the Chicago Bears when they won the National Football League's Super Bowl in 1986. Born in Camden, Larry Doby became the first African-American athlete to play baseball in the American League in 1947.

The Darlington NASCAR track is often called the "Granddaddy" of speedways for its 1,366 miles of track.

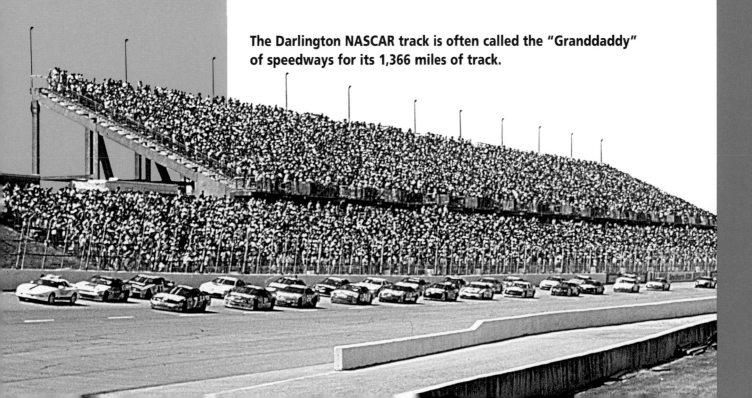

Brain Teasers

1

MULTIPLE CHOICE:

What is the official state dance of South Carolina?

a. the hustle

b. the shag

c. the waltz

d. the square dance

Answer: b. The official state dance of South Carolina is the shag. The square dance is the official folk dance of the state.

2

What interesting structure is found at Huntington Beach State Park?

Answer: Atalaya, the former home of sculptor Anna Hyatt Huntington, has a 40-foot tower. This fifty-five-room mansion is now open to the public.

3

Which South Carolina native was killed in 1986 when the Space Shuttle Challenger exploded?

Answer: Astronaut Ron McNair, from Lake City, was on the Challenger when it exploded on January 28, 1986.

4

MULTIPLE CHOICE:

What is the state song of South Carolina?

a. "South Carolina on My Mind"

b. "Carolina"

c. "Sweet Home Carolina"

d. "My Carolina"

Answer: Both a. and b. In 1911, "Carolina" was declared the state song of South Carolina. In 1984, "South Carolina on My Mind" was designated an official state song.

5

MULTIPLE CHOICE:

In which South Carolina city was U.S. President Andrew Jackson born?

a. Charleston

b. Columbia

c. Jackson

d. Waxhaw

Answer: d. Jackson was born in Waxhaw on March 15, 1767.

6

MULTIPLE CHOICE:

Which state grows more peaches than South Carolina?

a. California

b. Florida

c. Arizona

d. North Carolina

Answer: a

7

MULTIPLE CHOICE:

Which of the following competitions are held at the annual Sun Fun Festival at Myrtle Beach in South Carolina:

a. Bubble Gum Blowing Contest

b. Watermelon Eating Contest

c. Sandcastle Building Contest

d. all of the above

Answer: d

8

MULTIPLE CHOICE:

Which of the following civil-rights leaders is from South Carolina?

a. Jesse Jackson

b. Martin Luther King

c. Malcolm X

Answer: a

FOR MORE INFORMATION

Books

Fradin, Dennis Brindell. *South Carolina*. Chicago: Children's Press, 1994.

Howard, Blair. *Adventure Guide to the Georgia and Carolina Coasts*. Boston: Hunter Publishing, 1997.

Leacock, Elspeth. *The Southeast*. Washington, D.C.: National Geographic Society, 2002.

Web Sites

You can also go online and have a look at the following Web sites:

State of South Carolina
www.myscgov.com/

South Carolina Department of Parks, Recreation and Tourism
www.travelsc.com

South Carolina's Information Highway
www.sciway.net/

Some Web sites stay current longer than others. To find other South Carolina Web sites, enter search terms such as "Charleston," "Myrtle Beach," "Columbia," or any other topic you want to research.

GLOSSARY

blockaded: the closing off of a port or city in order to prevent entrance or exit

improvisation: performing without previous preparation

interactive: two-way communication that is capable of responding to each other

justice: a judge who presides over a court of law

parasailing: the sport of soaring while harnessed to a parachute-like device that is attached to a motorboat

patents: exclusive rights granted to inventors or companies to manufacture and sell an invention

persecution: the act of harassing or being harassed because of one's beliefs

pharmaceuticals: prescription drugs and medicines

plantations: large estates where crops are grown

pop artist: a twentieth-century artist who uses everyday objects, such as soup cans, as his or her subject matter

ratify: to approve

rural: of, or living in, the country

secede: to formally withdraw

segregation: forcing separation and restrictions based on race

steeplechase: a horse race over a turf course with artificial ditches, fences, and other obstacles over which the horses must jump

synthetic: prepared or made artificially, not of natural origins

urban: living in the city

INDEX